Dedication

To my daughter, you are full of kindness, compassion and courage for someone so small.
You show me the world is a better place through your eyes.
You are my sun, my moon and all my stars.
Love Mama

This is Alyssa.
She loves the seaside,
So her Daddies took us

This is Mary.
She loves eating ice cream,

So when I saw the van in the park,
I bought her a Strawberry Dream.
I love Mary.

This is Andre.
We like to play in the woods,
We chase through the leaves

and he saved me from Big Foot.
I love Andre.

and we cheer for his goals.
I love Nicolai.

The heart warming children's book "I Love My Friends", a beautiful celebration of diversity, culture, and the pure innocence of childhood. In a world where differences often divide us, this book reminds us of a simple truth.

"I Love My Friends" invites young readers on a journey through a vibrant, inclusive world where everyone belongs. Through delightful illustrations and touching stories, children learn that our differences are what make us special. They see the world with pure, innocent eyes, free from judgment, and full of love.

This book is more than just a story; it's a powerful tool for teaching acceptance, empathy, and kindness. It shows that friendship knows no boundaries and that we can all learn from the way children embrace diversity with open hearts.

Perfect for bedtime reading or classroom discussions, "I Love My Friends" is a must-have for every family and educator who wants to foster a more inclusive and loving world. Let's teach our children that love sees no differences, only friends.

Join us in spreading the message of unity, acceptance, and love with "I Love My Friends". Because the world would be a better place if we all saw it through the eyes of a child.

Written by Aimee Kidwell
From one Parent to Another.

Printed in Great Britain
by Amazon